DEDICATION

I dedicate this book to my family. My family knows my strength and weakness and they are always there for me through thick and thin.

TABLE OF CONTENTS

Chapter 1- Marriage and Communication

Although it may seem like rather a basic function to exercise, it is often difficult to simply verbally communicate with each other within the marriage perimeter. Most people find that instead of effective communication, they tend to bicker and this of course is not healthy for the communication exercise neither is it good for the marriage. Get all the info you need here.

Learning how to communicate effectively and without any negative connotations or emotions will help to create an ideal platform for both parties to be comfortable in. the following are some effective ways to adopt or in some cases avoid in order being able to establish some form of effective communication within the relationship:

Avoid using the cold shoulder or silent treatment tool. This almost always never works and certainly does not help the situation at all.

There is definitely a need to speak at some point during this situation as most people would attest to the fact that they are sincerely unsure as to why there is a negative situation in the first place.

Therefore by actually taking the trouble to communicate clearly and effectively, both parties will be privy to the actual cause of the current ugly situation and then will be able to move forward in a productive and positive manner.

Learning how to communicate with respect for each other is another very important element to include in the communicating exercise. Making unpleasant and degrading remarks will only contribute negatively to an already unpleasant situation.

Therefore in trying to get the concerns across and understood, there should be some level of dignity and respect present in the choice of words used.

Trying to hurt the other party as much as possible may seem satisfactory for the movement but it is rarely a good long term solution and might even damage the relationship beyond repair.

Communication

Due to the busy lifestyle of most people it has become a rather normal practice to communicate within the marriage relationship by means other than actual verbal communication. This is a very dangerous habit to form as eventually both parties will take the time or make the effort to verbally communicate at all, and this certainly spells disaster.

The Seed of Marriage

How to Stay In-Love and Committed

By: Andrea Clarkson

9781635010497

PUBLISHERS NOTES

Disclaimer – Speedy Publishing LLC

This publication is intended to provide helpful and informative material. It is not intended to diagnose, treat, cure, or prevent any health problem or condition, nor is intended to replace the advice of a physician. No action should be taken solely on the contents of this book. Always consult your physician or qualified health-care professional on any matters regarding your health and before adopting any suggestions in this book or drawing inferences from it.

The author and publisher specifically disclaim all responsibility for any liability, loss or risk, personal or otherwise, which is incurred as a consequence, directly or indirectly, from the use or application of any contents of this book.

Any and all product names referenced within this book are the trademarks of their respective owners. None of these owners have sponsored, authorized, endorsed, or approved this book.

Always read all information provided by the manufacturers' product labels before using their products. The author and publisher are not responsible for claims made by manufacturers.

This book was originally printed before 2014. This is an adapted reprint by Speedy Publishing LLC with newly updated content designed to help readers with much more accurate and timely information and data.

Speedy Publishing LLC

40 E Main Street, Newark, Delaware, 19711

Contact Us: 1-888-248-4521

Website: http://www.speedypublishing.co

REPRINTED Paperback Edition: ISBN: 9781635010497

Manufactured in the United States of America

The following are some tips on how to go about ensuring that verbal communication is a vital part of the exchange within the confines of a healthy and happy marriage:

Setting aside a specific amount to time to focus on verbal communication is sometime very necessary for the couple to be able to maintain some level of intimacy through the communication exercise.

This time allotted gives both parties an opportunity to speak their minds and heart and make each other be understood in a non threatening manner.

Doing so an atmosphere that is both welcoming and comfortable without any distractions would be worth exploring as it will help to keep both parties focused on each other and on what is being said.

Preparing oneself to be able to communicate in a non combative manner is also important. Taking the trouble and effort to be loving and nurturing when communicating will encourage both parties to be more receptive to what is being discussed.

Using endearing terms and a lot of encouragement will also help to facilitate a better exchange. Maintaining the friendly and loving verbal exchange will allow for more things to be accomplished.

Listening is also part of being totally immersed in the verbal form of communication.

Without the ability to listen, both parties will not be able to understand the communication session and neither will any positive outcome be achieved. The ability to simply listen will clearly show respect for the other party.

Understanding Body Language

It is sometime necessary to be able to read into the body language of the other party to better understand what is going on and how to best deal with any surfacing situation. Learning how to read the various body language signs will also allow each party to better understand and interpret the partner's wants and needs and work accordingly to accommodate them as far as possible.

The following are some popular body language signs that can be used to tip off the other party as to the current mindset and general disposition of each other:

Eyes clamped shut, stiffness in the neck and shoulders generally depict an individual who is either upset or not really happy with something.

These signals can be used to effectively help to defuse any situation before it goes out of hand and to also help to divert the person's attention to something that is more pleasurable and less upsetting.

This often takes the individual experiencing negativity away from the offending situation and thus encouraging a better frame of mind.

It should be noted that not all body language signals are negative. When an individual is in a sexy mood there are also some subtle and not so subtle body language moves that will allow the other party to respond accordingly should they wish to.

This is important to learn as it will help bring the couple closer when such displays of body language attempts are well read and acted upon. In most cases when the response is favorable, the party using the body language skills to communicate will be so encouraged and happy, that they would in all likelihood make it worthwhile and pleasurable for the responding party. This of course will heighten the communication mode to a deeper and fulfilling experience.

Chapter 2- Marriage and Active Listening

Learning to be a good listener certainly has its advantages and more often than not it allows the individual to seem like a very caring and considerate person. This is definitely worth learning how to achieve as most people appreciate a good listener over a good talker.

Understanding that listening is anything but a passive activity is a good place to start. Neither is listening expected to be an activity that is neutral and nothing else.

In fact good listeners are able to come up with good workable solutions as they are able to understand and follow the various contributing factors to any particular situation being discussed.

Developing the skill of being able to listen carefully also allows the individual to "hear" things that are not really being verbalized and yet important enough to need attention.

Sometimes these unspoken bits of information can be more informative than what is actually being said through the conversation, and when these bits of information allow the listen to act in a manner that is both soothing and helpful to the speaker, a huge amount of positive effects can be experienced.

Good listeners are usually people who are able to eventually become wise people. Listening takes a certain level of restraint and thus allows the person to mull over the matter being verbalized before making any judgment calls or giving any response.

By simply listening, the person is actually allowing the other party to vent everything and anything until fully satisfied.

After this happens the person will then be more receptive to any advice or comments made, thus allowing for some type of solution to be made. Two people taking and trying to get the thoughts and views across will not in any way help an already delicate situation.

Be Sensitive in What You Say and Hear

Sometime the wrong words are used or perhaps the wrong tone and this can create a situation that would otherwise not been forthcoming. Therefore in the quest to be clear and understood, the onus in on the individual to be as precise as possible with what is being verbalized.

Sometimes it is necessary to be assertive in both manner and choice of words in order for the individual to be taken seriously. Without being loud or rude, it is possible to ensure whatever is being verbalized is to be taken seriously and not to be disregarded as unimportant or frivolous.

Being clear in stating one's needs and wants is also something that should be encourage within a healthy relationship, as this will give both parties the opportunity to learn and respect the other's way of thinking and perception of things.

Avoid getting into the habit of depending on people reading between the lines or anticipating one's needs. This will most likely lead to a huge amount of disappointment and eventual annoyance when things don't go accordingly.

Learning not to apologize for certain feelings and thoughts is also something that should be encouraged as those who consistently back down will eventually not be taken seriously at all.

However when trying to communicate, it would be advisable to keep all emotions in check and also to speak clearly and firmly without unnecessary heights of volume included.

Respect is something that is very important to acquire when being clear about what is required as those who are unable to win the respect of others will not be taken seriously at all.

Sometimes it is necessary to repeat the request in order to ensure the items verbalized is properly understood and complied with. This will allow the other party to understand the importance of the matter verbalized and respect its boundaries.

Using a Touch While Talking

Most humans need to be touched especially within the perimeters of a healthy and happy relationship. Without the important touching factor constantly being exercised, both parties will eventually feel the missing ingredient and this could lead to some detrimental results.

Touching and being touched is something every healthy relationship should experience daily and as frequently as possible. The need for touch is very primal and basic, and stroking this desire will leave both parties feeling cherished and fulfilled.

It should be understood that not all touching should ideally lead to some form of sexual activity, as this is not only pressurizing but also quite unnecessary.

The act of touching should primarily be exercised as way to convey love, intimacy, comfort, happiness and any other positive connotations which are healthy for relationships.

A loving physical gesture can go along way and some say further than the spoken word. A lot of people respond well to the physical touch as long as there is no sexual connotation to it, unless the touch was specifically meant to be so.

Most people are simply unaware of the huge effects a simple touch can convey, thus often making the serious mistake of not incorporating the touch action into the everyday lives within a relationship.

Most marriages on the verge of collapse will usually concur on the fact that there was almost relatively no touching within the relationship, unless sex was the agenda.

This is rather a sad scenario, to live with, as touching does say a lot about the feelings of love and closeness of the couple within the relationship.

Even when having a simple conversation with the other party, some touching could be initiated to help the person relax and be more receptive to what is being said.

The Importance of Communication

In order to have a strong and healthy marriage most people would have to put in the appropriate amount of effort into the building process. This building process is usually an ongoing effort that should not be taken for granted at any given time.

Committing to good communication will also allow the couple to resolve issues before they become out of control problems.

Good communication skill will allow both parties to put forth their individual views without resorting to under handed measures such as insults and other negative verbal expressions.

Being able to fine tune the art of mutually beneficial conversation will certainly help prepare the couple for times when confrontations surface, as the previous ability to converse well, will help to keep both of them focused on resolving the matter in the most amicable way.

Committing to good communication will also help both parties to explore and find suitable solutions as quickly as possible rather than lingering on the problem.

In doing so the problem can be contained and there is less chances of it escalating and taking over the lives of both parties.

There are several different reasons as to the importance of committing to having a good and sound communication platform within a marriage.

This is sometimes the only means of keeping the marriage alive and well, especially if one party is unable for age or medical reasons to indulge in any sexual activity.

Being able to have a good conversation with each other is very refreshing and enlightening.

This is even more important as the marriage advances in years and there are no distractions such as children and jobs to occupy their time. In such instances being able to communicate will and on an exciting level will help to keep the marriage in good shape.

CHAPTER 3- EXPECTATION ON YOU FIRST YEAR OF MARRIAGE

Surviving your first year of marriage when you are a new couple can be challenging, especially if you are still learning about the other person. Generally, it is better to get to know someone before getting married but we all know this isn't how things happen in life. You meet someone special who melts your heart and next thing you know, you're head over heels for them. Already, you've been thinking of getting married and rush into things too soon. We've seen it so many times before with couples all over the world. Get all the info you need here.

If the two of you have not even lived together yet, there is a good chance that arguments will occur later in the relationship once you guys move in together. We often see this in many situations. It's actually referred to as the "stages" in your relationship.

Each relationship goes through a stage, no matter how close you are to the person. You might be nit-picky person who prefers everything spotless while your partner just throws his garbage wherever he is standing.

Other issues may arise such as times for intimacy, working late, going out with friends, and how you handle business around the house. All of these things can contribute to how the two of you get along. Rules should be established so that way you both can live happily married.

Marriage isn't just trying to survive. It is more meaningful then that. Marriage is about making sacrifices for the one that you truly love.

When they are sick, you make time away from work to take care of them. If your partner is upset about you going out a lot and not paying attention to them, you should give them more of your time. Doing small things can be a big help and make the relationship less dramatic in the sense of arguments.

Make sure you let your spouse know how much they mean to you each day and never take them from granite. You never know when you will see them again and this is why it's so important.

Communication skills are one of the most important aspects of marriage. If you can't communicate with your other half, the relationship is doomed. Try talking less and listening more. Or if you are someone who talks more and listens less, it is time to lend them your ear. Maybe your spouse wants you to listen to them so that way you'll know exactly how they feel about a certain situation.

The Seed of Marriage
Survival and marriage

In order to survive marriage, you need to know what your priorities are first. Work should never be your first priority, although your parents might say so otherwise. Your spouse should always come first. After all, they are the person that shares the home with you, cooks meals, makes extra money for your both, helps watch the kids, and be intimate from time to time.

There are so many activities to do in marriage and in this age, usually both people are working. This is what makes the marriage so difficult because men are not used to doing activities that a woman would be doing. For example, most men refuse to iron their laundry or clean the bathroom. It really isn't something they would do. And forget planting flowers out in the backyard. They won't even go near the flowers.

Men are trained to work hard by their fathers and get a good education to provide for their family. They aren't the ones who can become pregnant and grow close to their child. Usually, once the mother has given birth is when they become emotional. A man needs to see their child in order to believe the reality of the matter. They do not understand what women go through during pregnancy and expect us to do everything around the house.

Woman is generally more emotional and seems to talk more than doing household work. If the toilet leaks or the sink is broken, guess who they call? They call their husband in a panic. The woman are good at doing chores such as folding laundry, cooking a delicious meal, and getting all dressed up for that dance their husband is taking them to after work.

Eventually, at the end of the day - both man and woman are in the same bed. The woman is reading her book, focused intently on what she is reading. The man can only thing about one thing and that's sexual intimacy. This is the only time he begins to talk to her, trying romance and even rubbing her.

Sometimes it works and sometimes it doesn't. When men do get their way, they usually climb on top and do their job. After, their spouse just lies there, trying to catch her breath.

The problem is that the man already falls asleep without saying I love you or anything that shows appreciation. It is like nothing ever happened. Obviously, this is because most men aren't emotional and they just do things whenever they like.

Dividing everyday activities and trying to spend time together on an emotional or physical level can be challenging. Currently, this is why couples are heading straight toward divorce. It's because they don't know how to communicate and be fair to their spouse. It only takes cooperation, listening, and a little empathy when it comes to the other person.

Difficulties of the first marriage

There are many difficulties when it comes to marriage. The most popular are expectations, intimacy, connection and money. All of these topics can contribute to a problem. The husband may spend a lot of money on his gambling habits while the wife is upset and just wants him to stop. They need that money for their children.

Another example is for the woman. She is often too busy doing things around the house that she becomes stressed and sex is the last thing on her mind. However, the husband highly values intimacy and without it, he may feel as if he is growing apart from his wife.

The Seed of Marriage

You see, it's all the little things that will add up to cause a husband and wife to start arguing. They may be resentful toward one another and not want to work things out with each other. Some may try but sometimes the other person isn't as cooperative as they are. This is what makes relationships so difficult. Here are the four difficulties when it comes to marriage:

Expectations

The wife has such high expectations for you when you get home. She doesn't want you to leave your towel on the floor and also won't let you eat in your own room, out of fear that there will be crumbs on the bed. This doesn't make you thrilled at all. As for you, you expect your wife to always have dinner ready by the time you come home and to look her best. This is all you really care about.

Intimacy

If you've been craving intimacy for a few weeks and your husband is too tired to do anything with you, it is important to understand how he feels. Instead of pressuring him, give him a soft backrub that shows you care. He may be under a lot of stress from work. When it comes to intimacy, it works both ways for men and women.

Connection

Connecting with your other half is very important. If the two of you have a deep connection, there is no room for divorce or a split up. Most couples who are connected with each other tend to understand one another better. Sympathy and empathy in the relationship go hand in hand. If their partner is sad then they are. Sometimes it may take a few years for a couple to feel truly connected with each other or less than a few months, depending on how long they've been together.

Money

Sadly, financial issues are one of the top reasons for divorce. If the two of you have trouble handling money and bills tend to pile up, the relationship will become strained. It is strained because of the stress that's accumulated during financial hardships.

Chapter 4- How to Manage Your First Year Challenges

Being married has many benefits and if you stay together to work on problems that arise, the relationship will grow stronger. Keep in mind that both of you will want to work on marriage problems.

Only if one person is willing to go to counseling or talk to you about the issues of the marriage, it will be a one way street. This means the marriage won't be able to progress.

It is important to let your other half know why you want certain habits in the relationship to change. Tell him/her you are serious and if things don't change, that you may very well file for divorce.

Your spouse will see that you are talking business and will want to change some of their habits. Of course - don't be surprised if when the two of you sit down, they talk about some of the things you do. It is also okay for them to address your bad habits when you it comes to marriage.

Solutions

Solutions are fairly easy to come up with in a marriage but sticking to those solutions isn't always easy. This is what the two of you must overcome and if one of you has trouble sticking to your goals, then communication is necessary.

The other person might come to reality and let you know they just cannot change, even though they have tried. Some people are at a spot in their lives where they really don't want to change. Something must fuel their strong desire to change. Most of the time, this desire is to keep you and make their family life better.

You should understand that with possible marriage solutions, not every idea you come up with will work. For example, if you decide to have separate bank accounts because of your wife's spending habits - she might even beg you to borrow her money. This creates tension on the marriage, because you see her habits unfolding once again and this leads to an argument.

Maybe it's not the wife this time. Your husband often visits raunchy strip clubs and leaves you at home. His excuse is that you never are intimate with him.

Let him know it is not okay to do this and the next time he does it, you should leave for a few days. Once you come back, focus on the intimacy in your relationship. Are you too tired to be intimate with him? Focus on his needs earlier, before you both go to bed. Make it fun and don't act like it's a chore. We bet that the both of you enjoyed each other when you first entered the relationship, right? By bringing him back to this time, he will appreciate you and stay home more often. If he doesn't, it may be time to let it go as this really wasn't his excuse to go out.

Education

Do you know the types of education for early marriages? There are about five stages of marriage where the couple gets to know each other, face problems, argue, get over these problems, focus on children, and become successful in their marriage.

The majority of the time, this will take many years. However, some couples are blessed from the get-go. They were friends for such a long time that they know the habits of their spouse and no longer have to work at the marriage. Everything seems to come alive by itself. When this happens, it is an apparent that the two of you are closely bonded.

Now, if you are experiencing relationship problems, you may be in the early stage of "reality". At this stage, you are just getting to know how they act in certain situations. You may see your husband or wife at their worst when they are angry or upset. This can be a scary situation, especially if you have not seen these types of emotions from your partner before. Much of the time, this will cause arguments down the road.

Let's go ahead and look at some of the types of education for early marriages and how each stage unfolds:

The Honeymoon Stage - Almost always in the honeymoon stage, couples are extremely excited about one another and the romance seems to just take off on its own. This is because they aren't experiencing any problems in life. Most couples engage in fun sexual activities with one another and will also enjoy basking in romance. This is a time when couples go out for dinner with each other, exercise together, and go to parties together. The honeymoon stage can either be before the wedding or after it, on their honeymoon. It really depends on the length of time you've known the person.

Reality Stage - At this stage, some couples feel lost and will even compare their partners with a past boyfriend or girlfriend. They begin to feel that the relationship is a mistake and they might not be compatible with that person. Feelings of sadness, disappointment and even anger can surface. This is perfectly normal and the reason why couples go through this is because problems are starting to peak through. When a couple is very close with one another, they'll often see the "bad" characteristics of that person. This leaves the other person distraught and unsure of what to do in the relationship. Most of the time. Normally, the reality stage lasts up until two years.

Family Stage - The relationships becomes closer in childbearing years due to some of the conflicts that may area. Instead of the focus being on the marriage itself, everything is directed toward the kids. The man and woman work harder to reach their goals, instead of going out on a romantic date. They realize that planning a family involves a lot of preparation.

Once they have a child together, they'll become closer as a couple in order to try and make their child happy. Problems such as the baby crying, hospital visits and financial issues may arise at this time but by now - you both will know how to handle it once the reality stage as passed.

The Seed of Marriage
The success stage- If the two of you have been together for ten years or more, there is a good chance you have completed the success stage. Usually when your children become a teenager or an adult, you've gone through everything there is to go through possibly in a marriage. It is safe to say you have found a life partner where the two of you will be there until the very end. Congratulations!

The Newly Married Couples

Are you newly married and want to know the basic soft skills you'll need in order to progress through the marriage? In order to do this, you cannot ask too much from your partner and communication is the key. Accepting your partner how she/he behaves is very important.

You can always talk about any bad habits or behavior later, but wait until counseling. For now, it's better for the both of you to fight once in awhile and come to terms with annoying in-laws. If there are more than a couple problems, you can address them all at once.

Love

The number one thing that holds a relationship together is unconditional love for the other person. If you love them for their personality rather then what they look like, there is a good chance the two of you will go far in life. Your wife could be an incredibly gorgeous looking woman and later become bigger because of the last two children she blessed you with.

In another instance, you absolutely adore your handsome husband but something has changed his life. He was recently attacked by a bear, leaving him scarred everywhere.

The two of you grew closer and even though he has scars on his face and some disfigurement, you still love him for his personality. He's always been a funny and outgoing guy. Give him lots of love and appreciate that he's still around. Remember that is attack could have been so severe that it would have been fatal.

What to expect

Whatever you do, it's not a good idea to nag on your partner or expect too much. This can be extremely stressful on them. It is better to encourage them and give them suggestions at this point.

By doing this, you will help them grow as a person and develop better habits. If your guy was messy before he even met you, there might have been some small changes. Instead of throwing his coat on the floor - he picks it up. This is obviously a mark of progress but don't expect him to clean the whole house or do laundry.

Communication

Talking with your spouse is very important. If the two of you can't discuss important problems, issues, or dates within the relationship - consider the marriage over.

You might still be in the reality stage of your marriage and in this case, you are just getting to know that your partner is very shy around people. If he is shy around you, give him a slight push.

You'll need to do this by asking him questions and talking about anything that comes to mind. In time, he'll come around so try not to worry so much about it.

CHAPTER 5- THE HARD CHALLENGES DURING THE FIRST YEAR OF MARRIAGE

Marriage can be a beautiful thing but incorporating hard skills into a new marriage isn't something that everyone wants to do. However, you must do this in order to make sure the marriage progresses. If you don't, the marriage will be doomed and you'll practically have nothing to work with.

Remember that Earth was created for humans to interact with each other and most of our life revolves around family memories. This is absolutely precious to us.

Family should always come first instead of going out with friends, working too much, or stressing over small things that do not have any direction towards the relationship. Take it slow and enjoy your time. Always be firm with your partner by incorporating hard skills into the relationship. Here are a few you'll want to learn about:

Problem solving

Whenever the two of you want to go eat out, it is a constant battle. For example, he enjoys eating food from South America while you only like to eat sushi. He absolutely hates sushi and anything with fish or rice with soy sauce isn't something he would like to eat. This leaves you feeling distressed when it's finally time to eat out.

How about going to two different restaurants to get what both of you want? You can order take out and go eat it at home, or plan a romantic dinner at the park. If you want to eat at a real restaurant though, just bring your food with you that you bought from the other restaurant. The two of you will be happy and won't argue anymore with this type of technique. As you can see, problem solving in a marriage is very important.

Put your spouse first

This is probably the most difficult thing to do since most of us are generally selfish beings. However, if you love your spouse - you should do this for them. Find out what they want.

You can always make room for your needs on a different day. If they are feeling stressed, sad, or angry - talk with them. Ask your spouse if you can do anything to make he/she feel better. They will start to develop more respect toward you.

Be a forgiver

Many times in relationships, the wife or husband does something wrong that upsets the others. This leaves feelings of disappointment, anger, despair or even sadness.

The Seed of Marriage
Hold your feelings back and talk to them about why they did what they did. If it is an issue with cheating, you'll need to know why they did this to you. Many times when people cheat, their spouse is not giving them what they need.

The most apparent reason is for lack of intimacy or lack of emotions. People will have an emotional or physical affair, depending on what problems are within the marriage. Instead of getting upset, just let them know how hurt you are and you want to make it work. Give them at least one more chance.

Survival on Your First Year

Surviving marriage has great benefits for couples. Some of them include growing as a person, become more loving, being able to express your issues with your other half, and even becoming financially stable with the two of you working.

Marriage vows entail being together forever and you should be there for your spouse at all times. By doing so, you will become a mentally healthy person and will also help them as well.

Kids can greatly benefit from your marriage as we all know what anger does to kids when their parents experience divorce. Do yourself a favor and don't let them go through this. Taking your time to make it work is the best thing for your future. Don't give up!

Here are a few benefits of marriage survival below:

Being happy in life

When you are with someone you truly love, you'll become a happier person in life. After all, they are there to share laughter with you, cheer you up, or accompany you in times of sadness. If you are going for frequent hospital visits for cancer, you might feel anxiety but if your other half is there to support you - you will have a much better day. This is just one example of what we are talking about. By having a partner, you won't go through certain situations alone. Unfortunately, some people who are widowed or recently divorced become bitter and uncaring towards others.

Protecting your children

By staying in your marriage, you are protecting your children. For example, many girls who do not have fathers will most likely become pregnant at a young age or fall into a rebellious attitude which could result in drug use or drinking. A father is there to provide love, discipline, and protection to anything that could harm his daughter.

Also, some kids will develop depression after seeing their parents split up. Our kids are incredibly precious and you'll want to make sure they are okay. Seeing a kid grow up with sadness in their heart is something that could very well tear a parent apart. Most of the time, we would do anything for our kids to be happy. There is a greater chance of this if they children have seen their parents together for a long time. It may be a confusing and sad year for them. It doesn't last for a year but can scar a child in life.

Become financially stable

Usually, it takes two people to support a household. If you happen to have kids, this makes matters worse. A single mother working one job may not be able to make it through because of the bills, the cost of a child, and surprise hospital visits. She might even get evicted from the home because of falling behind. However, with two people working - you will become financially stable. As long as the other person and yourself handle money well and take care of bills like you should, the two of you will be fine.

Make sure your partner doesn't have a gambling problem and always look over your bank account statements to see what's going on. You never know when money could "disappear". This could be from identity theft or your spouse may be taking money from you for their poor spending habits. Sharing a bank account together should only be done once you have been together after a few years and trust them.

First Year Marriage Tips

Here are the A-Z marriage secrets and tips for a successful marriage for newly-weds.

Advice

Offering advice to your partner in times of stress or problems is a great way to make the marriage really work. Often, they won't take out their problems on you. Instead, they'll feel the need to open their heart and talk about the problems. If you can offer your spouse advice, they'll be grateful that they are with you. Don't know how to give advice? No problem. You can always give them a backrub and just hold them. Ask them more questions about the issue to make it look like you are really interested in the problems they are going through. Most men don't want to hear every detail of their spouse's day. A few details are fine but when you over-do it, they can become overwhelmed and won't know what to say.

Devotion

Being devoted to your partner means seeing them on a regular basis, making date nights happen, and spending time no matter how busy you are. If you have a small window to be with them on your day off, then go for it! If your love is in the hospital and hasn't been able to walk for a month, visit them often. Bring him/her flowers and tell them how much you love them. Showing your devotion will have them realize how much you care for them and they'll develop a strong bond with you. These types of relationships will blossom into something more and they tend to last for years at a time.

Honesty

If you are someone who is already honest, this may come easy for you. Did you have a wild party at home and all your buddies decided it would be funny to draw on your white wall? You had no idea this had happened, even when you got home. Your husband told you that your son was the one who drew on the walls. However, your son was at the party and taking pictures on his toy camera. Keep in mind, this camera actually processes films for kids. After finding all the pictures, you feel disappointed in what your husband did. As you can see here, being honest causes fewer problems in the relationship - even if it was your fault. If you cannot trust someone in the relationship, you will always be second guessing their actions in your mind. This is obviously not very healthy for you or your partner. You don't want to accuse them of doing something wrong. Maybe they never did anything wrong and you are the one who owes them the apology. See what happens when honesty isn't within the relationship? It just makes it worse.

Intimacy

Did you know that intimacy and love goes together? While some woman might not think this, men will consider intimacy in the bed as a form of love. They believe it is sexually healing. Most men become closer to their wives after making love. Also, for woman, foreplay is extremely important. Men need to know this too. If you rush this with your wife, she may feel that you do not love or appreciate her body. Take your time and have fun. You'll enjoy the experience more.

Laughter

Laughing with your partner is fun and even invites you both to "play" together. Remember the time when you pushed your partner in the pool when he was wearing all his clothes? He wasn't happy at the time but the both of you laughed about it later. The pictures you took of him with his shocked expression while falling as simply hilarious. He couldn't help but laugh at everything that had happened. Giving each other tickles and even making fun of one another is always a great way to put a smile on your face. Every time the two of you laugh, you are creating memories that will last a lifetime. By laughing, you are pushing away anything in your life that is bad. Laughter is a form of healing as well.

Parenting

Being a good parent to your children is very important. The way you treat your children also affects your spouse. If you are a mother who is very stressed because your kids do not listen to you, there is a good chance you yell at the kids every once and awhile.

Your husband frowns upon this as he is a very calm and understanding man. Try to analyze to see what he does when the kids are acting up. Learn from him or learn from books on parenting. The way you parent your children will affect them for the rest of your life and believe it or not - you affect those around you in a chain reaction.

In order to find permanent solutions for your marriage, you will need to start doing some problem solving. There should be a solution for every problem in marriage such as money issues, infidelity, parenting issues and so forth. Here are some permanent solutions to help you survive the marriage:

Concentrate on yourself

Believe it or not but this tactic works. Ask your partner what aggravates them when it comes to you and work on that attribute of yourself. If he/she say's you are too bossy, try calming down. Do some mind clearing exercises and learn how to do things on your own. By doing this, you are setting yourself up for a better relationship. You won't rely on what he/she does and can get most of the stuff done.

Don't expect too much

When you expect too much from your spouse, they will become miserable in the relationship. It is possible they will feel resentful toward you and this may result in infidelity, arguments, or you they might even move away from you slowly.

Speak with a counselor

Talking to a counselor is better than arguing over the smallest problems. Each side can be heard and you won't have to worry about this type of communication blowing up into an argument. The counselor will be able to go over some of the progress are gaining as a couple and things may get better then they were before.

Chapter 6- Long Lasting Marriage

Unhappy people who think that ending their marriage would make them more pleased are frequently living a myth. Chances are that they've ascribed the failure of the marriage to their mate, relinquishing introspection. Blaming the other rather than oneself becomes the favorite pursuit, the handiest means to walk away.

By failing to admit their own debilities, and not recognizing that they've entered the marriage with absurd demands and unrealistic expectations, they unconsciously freed the forces leading to a likely separation.

There's likewise the phenomenon of short memories. Somehow, the same people who vowed to support one another have forgotten their commitment and vows to love one another through thick and thin.

Our modern society has become a disposable society. When our once dear partner is no more of use to us, we call our attorney and instruct him/her to initiate a divorce.

The Seed of Marriage
Truth is, is that divorce has an atrocious side to it. It's the simple way out for individuals who haven't an ounce of bravery to salvage what deserves to be salvaged.

Divorce un-builds and unties what took years to nourish, and sadly, frequently the only individuals who benefit from it are greedy attorneys who will utilize every trick in the book to strip the other assets, till no remnant of the person's investment - physical, monetary and emotional - persists.

While divorcing couples spend their mental energies charging the other with causing anguish and disharmony, they forget that the youngsters suffer in double - triple doses. Couples blank out that the sentiments of youngsters are more delicate and harder to mend. This is when the concept of human selfishness and self-interest become transparent. It's odd how the true character of individuals comes out when they're the actors in a divorce.

The conclusion not to be swayed by the lows of a relationship mirrors strength and integrity, let alone the power to see beyond one's personal sadness. And by saving the marriage, more than one human is saved.

This is the essence of this e-book in your hands right now; maybe the most crucial that you'll ever read.

Getting married is entering into a contract - but it's likely the one contract that's the easiest to break because divorce has made it simple for husband and wife to walk out when they go through a distressed period in their life, albeit impermanent.

Just think - attorneys will fight tooth and nail to protect businesses in their contract relations or between you and your landlord, your auto-mechanic and your physician, but can't prevent you from breaking up with your mate. In fact, they'd even counsel you to break up your marriage and then discuss division of belongings as the next logical step.

Marriage is the sole contract that anybody can break, at any time, and not be held responsible for it.

From a cost position, divorce may be economically damaging not only for the state but likewise for couples.

Think about these figures:

US divorces cost the nation $33 billion annually or $312.00 per home;

The average divorce in America costs state and federal authorities $30,000 in direct and indirect costs. Direct costs to the state include youngster support enforcement, Medicaid payments, temporary assistance to needy families fund (TANF), food stamps and housing project assistance.

To the couple, divorce costs about $18,000 and this would include lost work productiveness, relocation costs and legal fees that vary vastly, depending upon the nature of the divorce and the state of affairs of the couple.

There are other reasons why divorced individuals don't end up happier:

Depression symptoms do not necessarily diminish with divorce, nor did divorce raise people's self-esteem;

Unhappy marriages were less common than unhappy spouses.

It all boils down to mental attitude, doesn't it? Cynics have named marriage the "old ball and chain." Many happily wedded individuals disagree, as they don't view marriage as bondage and slavery, where one's innate instincts and desires have to play second fiddle to the felicity of the other half.

Happily wedded couples state that marriage has taught them to accept each other's fortes and possibilities. They argue that by exercising that, they transform themselves from the average to the extraordinary.

Marriage consequently is an "enabling" sort of situation where it means the freedom to be who they truly are, to reach for the stars and discover what they're meant to be without ridicule or rejection.

A lot of us have read reports that deliver the message: married individuals are healthier and happier, and hence live longer than single or celibate mortals.

For one, there's the emotional support they get when the going gets rough, and the fact that married life supplies the opportunities to maintain communication between two individuals, even if one of the mates just wishes to vent. In fact among the reasons individuals say they like being married is the assurance that there's somebody they may come home to at the end of a difficult day.

"For better or for worse" is yet very much a strong argument for getting - and remaining - married. While some individuals would be too shy to admit it, the love and support in times of sickness may speed up recovery.

People in fact like the "for better or for worse" aspect of wedlock because it tells them that regardless what occurs, somebody will be around.

It goes beyond having a surety or safety net. It's the knowledge that they may count on somebody when times are tough, and that alone returns a considerable degree of peacefulness and a sense of calm for the soul.

And here's a romantic - but real - notion of wedlock, to which happily married couples will concur: "Marriage moves us from ego to we-go.

The single self switches from me first to the sacred union of us...values like love, honesty, regard, fidelity and dependability form the engine of a great marriage. Little benignities are the oil. Without the oil, it will grind. With it, it slides."

And how about the barest reasons for marriage like: cockamamie little jokes, hugs and cuddling, traveling together, expressing joy together, quiet times together, mutual acquaintances, sexual intimacy, pillow talk, kissing and making up? Can anybody truly put a price tag on these simple pleasures? Don't they echo the saying that the finest things in life are free?

Oh yes, there is love in relationships, but there's deeper love in a marriage that is on its way to its 25th or 50th year. Individuals who have remained happily married are those who recognize gradually that there are really two marriage contracts, not simply one.

The 1st contract is what everybody is acquainted with - the one that the clergyman in a wedding ceremony makes official. The 2nd contract is what couples call the silent contract. It's secret, implicit and mostly unconscious. It's this 2nd contract that assigns standards and behaviors our partner ought to fulfill.

The distinctive feature of this contract is our secret belief that our own feelings, needs, and sense of what is correct are most crucial. One's expectations of the other may carry risks and may lead to clashes, which couples attempt to resolve among themselves.

Regrettably, as mentioned earlier, these conversations are seldom objective or profitable, given that people rarely ask if their expectations are fair and sensible - they simply complain endlessly.

Happily married couples are those who comprehend this 2nd silent contract and all of its ramifications.

Happily married couples are those who carry on investing in the marriage, knowing that for love to prosper, it takes hard work and hearty amounts of creative thinking.

Love and physical attraction might take the backseat, particularly when the youngsters arrive, but fulfilled couples know that they have to stick it out, through thick and thin, for the sake of the emotional welfare of the youngsters.

When couples consider others and not just themselves and make a continuing attempt to make the marriage work, they've made the best investment they may ever make and they firmly trust in this.

The motivation to make the partnership work is frequently the secret of happy marriages.

Foundation of Marriage

Friends are forever. Even if we move out of town or move abroad, we preserve our friendships.

We surely don't divorce our friends just because of a misinterpretation, so if we treated our mate as a dear friend, we likely won't ever need a divorce attorney and go through the awful exercise of property division - a course that may spell financial downfall for many.

As love is less permanent (we fall in and out of love a few times in our life) and friendship more lasting, every attempt has to be made to make our mate not only a lover and a partner, but likewise a friend.

Friendship is apparent manifestation of maturity. Marriage is an obligation larger than life, and may be a source of bother or profound joy. Only when we turn those bothers and joys into building blocks for a lasting friendship can we say that we've taken the unbendable path to a marriage made in heaven.

If there's true friendship between husband and wife, the marriage wards off landing on the rocks. Rather it becomes a rock-hard marriage where no person or circumstance may put it asunder.

As a matter of fact, it's the genuine friendship between two individuals that put more meaning in the words, "for richer or for poorer, for better or for worse, till death do us part".

Friendship in a marriage implies that the marriage will be fraught with memories of laughter and humor, for didn't we pick those friends who made us laugh the most? Didn't our mothers forever tell us, "When picking out a husband, count the times he made you laugh."

Friendship likewise means open and honest communicating; a no holds barred type of union where our comfort level with our mate goes beyond 100%, assured that what we say and how we say it won't be labeled or taken in a damaging light.

If you speak to married individuals, a wish they frequently express is that they stay the best of friends and the closest of companions. Surveys in point of fact reveal that if there's one component that will enable a couple to brave the tough times, it's friendship.

As a celebrated poet once stated, "No man is an island." friendship is the counter poison to loneliness. Getting married doesn't mean that individuals will never go through loneliness, "but it does decrease our sense of separateness.

Friendship between couples yields wholesome feelings of goodwill and fidelity. Our mate - our friend - has our interests at heart, won't betray us and will be our most steadfast supporter. Friendship likewise makes spouses solider; this strength is reinforced by the delight of shared history, of nostalgia and designs for the future.

Romance is a great thing, and we could utilize heaps of it when our relationships become rocky. But mature friends know that romance may be a barrier to friendship.

How come? Because romance hides the darker side of our existence - our fears, anxieties, and insecurities. Yet, it's those concerns, anxieties and insecurities that by nature draw us to our friend.

Friendship in a marriage produces the recognition that flux, de-stabilization and disturbance are the first steps in the dynamic procedure of repair, reconstructing and replenishment.

Familiarity doesn't breed contempt. It breeds content. A sensation of contentment equates with satisfaction, fondness, and unwavering assurance. Sharing a life together in love and friendship makes for a book that has deeper and thicker in shared stories, in content.

If you were to ask a happy unmarried man and a happily married man to each compose their stories, you'd get a favorable narration from both.

The single individual's perspective would however be I, me and myself - and perhaps a string of blind dates and Saturday nights lonely.

The married man will discuss "us", of mutual interests - an account definitely made richer because there are 2 stories, not one.

Chapter 7- Marriage and Family Security

The family is still an all-important unit of the community. When individuals get married, their hopes are linked to establishing a home and family.

Families are ancient institutions. Ever since humans cut across the savannas in search of food, our families have been unparalleled...

Homo sapiens need families to endure, and well done to those millions of parents who are attempting to do the correct thing.

Happily married individuals understand this very basic concept. It is not just their own core that needs caring, but the whole institution of marriage and the social unit called a family.

When marriages prosper, so do families, and as a result, communities everywhere in the world likewise flourish. That's how societies become more substantial and progressive. When the littlest unit survives, the larger ones survive.

I write of families as I love them. When I travel alone far from home, I consider my children's faces to calm myself. I picture them grinning, studying, playing. I picture my hubbies face bent over his guitar or relaxed and refreshed, the way it is on the mornings when we have coffee together. Those faces are my rock. They comfort and secure me. The faces of those we love are the first, the key, rocks for us all.

These are the views that happily married individuals nurture and have in their hearts. If they centered on their rocks rather than on their frustrations and unrealized wants, these are the individuals who have shown an unbelievable willingness of reaching out, of seeing past their own self-importance.

Marriage isn't the extension of the romance addict phase. It's equivalent to a long term commitment that emotionally smart husbands and wives comprehend totally.

They understand, deep in their hearts, that love and passion won't always be on the day-to-day agenda, and might diminish as the responsibilities of their marriage take them to the following level - family life.

Consider What You Do and Say

"Don't sweat the small stuff" is likely one piece of advice that doesn't always work for marriage, as it's crucial to notice the little stuff, if the marriage were to thrive. Most of the true work in relationships is happening in quieter moments in littler spaces.

Quashing bringing up the faulty garage door while your hubby is rushing to meet a deadline and needs to center on his project for a couple of hours; Attending the youngsters and keeping them away from the kitchen when your wife fixes supper;

The Seed of Marriage

Offering to get your hubbies shirts at the cleaners because he forgot to do it yesterday;

Filling up the car if you know that your hubby must drive out of town on a customer visit;

Taking your wife dancing as she's forever loved to dance even if you have 2 left feet and have always despised it.

One thorn in a marriage is income. Chances are mates have their own ways of spending and preserving money. If both husband and wife earn like wages, agree on how to split the home expenses before getting married so no one feels betrayed or deprived financially.

While it was fine to expect him to pay for supper and the film while you were going out, marriage demands a genuine economical partnership. Or, if you know that your hubby is especially averse to un-needed shopping sprees, make an effort to reduce your buying trips and center on the essentials rather than on your impulses. Don't forget to talk over your investment preferences and attempt to stick to a budget and a savings plan.

The same is truthful for sex and politics: if your hubby likes to watch porn as a prelude to making love, let him know that you're not especially in favor of this exercise but do indulge him at times. If your wife likes to visit temple and do charity work in her parish, don't convey any bitterness or complain that she's spending too much time on her fundraising actions.

Work at keeping your mate stimulated intellectually. If there's anything that grates, it's a married woman who constantly discusses what's on sale and a married man who knows nothing but what squads made it to the playoffs this year.

Look backward to wooing days when both of you could talk till the wee hours of the morning as you were interested in what each of you did in the office that day, or how the Dow-Jones Industrial Average sparkled as of news about Intel or Microsoft, and so forth.

Enrich one another with your experiences and vicarious lives. Let the other know that you've an interest in life and what it has to provide, and make every attempt not to be a boring better half by reading more, trying out more, and living more.

A lot of individuals say that youngsters put a damper on the union. Who has time for passion and love when the children are crying their lungs out or running a fever? Or once money has to be foraged for to pay for those expensive dental visits? Raising kids may turn us into impatient, stressed- out beings so if employing a sitter overnight won't disrupt the monthly budget, do so and leave - just the two of you.

But don't utilize that time away from kids to complain about each other's beliefs or to raise preceding incidents!

Rather than looking at marriage blessed with high points or fraught with depressed points, consider it instead as a series of landmarks. These landmarks have to be regarded as chances to make a marriage solider and more fulfilling. These landmarks become lucid at mid-life where couples have built up a keener sense of time limits and urgency in their want to make the most out of their union and their lives.

The mid-life years are an innate time for reflections: couples now have the benefit of being able to see where they've been, where they are and where they wish to go.

The Seed of Marriage

Provide credit where it's due, be generous with compliments and be earnest in your praise. Do you occasionally find yourself wishing that your mate would compliment you the way your boss does following a job well done? A lot of couples discover that as they settle into their union, the compliments or kind kudos are not as frequent as while they were dating.

Making it a pattern to provide credit where it's due and being sincere about your kudos go a long way toward reinforcing health in a marriage.

If you see that your wife works religiously on the treadmill to avoid the weight, did you ever think that she's likely doing this to please you? Saying something like, "You're in such good condition, I'm proud of you" will add to her confidence and reinforce her mental attitude that she's doing something that's healthy and that you value.

If your hubby is great at the budget, praise him for his skills. "You're astonishing with numbers" will give him a sense of pride, and he will feel significant to you.

Without doubt a lot of authorities and marriage counselors will differ in popular opinion on how to save a marriage, but they all concur on the accompanying key elements of a solid marriage - only the words and the way they're conveyed are changed:

Trust and communicating

Regard for each other's ideas and anticipations Faithfulness

Physical and intellectual arousal

Preserving their own personalities, but supporting each other's aspirations

Much as it sounds awfully outmoded, marriage is a commitment, and people have to make every attempt not to cheapen that commitment in any way. Remaining married is a lifelong effort.

It requires guts. It requires nerves of steel to make a marriage work. A sense of humor and a lower degree of ego may sustain us in that work.

The roadblocks will be numerous, and there will be spots where we'll question our saneness, unsure if we may really hang on.

It will be a massive effort to stay attracted to the same qualities that pulled you to your spouse on the first day you met. Your mate is still the same individual you fell in love with, he has not altered his soul, his being, only his jacket.

So if there's only way to split up, but a 1000 ways to save your union, which path will you pick? Are you going to fall by the wayside or adopt one more challenge?

There's very little substance to saving face or saving dollars; it's much worthier to save soul.

Chapter 8- Your Pre-Marriage Measures

The style of counseling is becoming more popular in current times and is usually popularly backed by various religions and governmental agencies. This is primarily some to create a better understanding and acceptance of what it entails to be part of a lasting relationship. The main idea behind this particular exercise is also to limit the possibility of a high divorce rate and to try and keep couple together as a family unit for the betterment of the children.

These counseling sessions are designed to help couples prepare for the eventual marriage as best as possible and with all the knowledge that they should ideally be equipped with. It is hoped that with these sessions, the couple heading for marriage will be stronger and more focused on making the marriage last. Giving the participants a better chance at achieving a stable and satisfying marriage is usually what forms the basis of the counseling sessions.

Another main aim of the counseling sessions is to help the couple intending to walk down the aisle a chance to identify weakness that are evident in each other and work toward either changing for the better or learning how to accept each other and move on. However this acceptance has to be complete and without compromise, so that it does not surface later to create problems within the relationship.

Couple who do not attempt to attend such counseling session may find that some of the problems that could have been identified and sorted out before the marriage actually takes place, would instead become the focal point of contention within the relationship and eventually cause enough damage to create discord and dissatisfaction within the relationship. This of course will usually end up causing such harm that divorce would not most likely present a good option to seek out.

Finances

Finances are usually a very delicate subject to approach and discuss especially if the couple are still in the early stages of the relationship. This is still difficult even when both parties are contemplating a more stable commitment with each other. A lot of questions should be asked and ideally a lot of good and intelligent answers should be given, as this will eventually give both parties a clear idea of how each individual handles money issues.

There are several different issues that should be discussed and the pre marital counseling session usually conducts such discussions to ensure both parties face the realities of financial elements within the eventual partnership. Some of the issues based on finances should include how each party sees and prioritizes financial choices made.

These could include payments towards accumulated debts, payments towards retirement plans, payments toward establishing an emergency fund and any other such payments which very few people consider and certainly even less actually start.

These are all very important financial commitments that would require the cooperation of both parties in order to ensure harmony within the relationship.

Other more simpler issues that should also be discussed within the pre marital counseling sessions on finances would be the seemingly simple daily expenses, weekly expenses and monthly expenses both parties are currently committed to or have grown accustomed to spending on.

These expenses may seem acceptable and even necessary to each individual but would most certainly not be shared by the other party. This could eventually be an area of contention if these feelings and perceptions are not discussed and understood by both individuals.

Coming up with a suitable budget together is also something that will be taught during these counseling sessions and it could prove to be very useful indeed as the advice given is usually from tried and true methods already successfully in use.

Family and Children

Most people tend to go into a relationship with preconceived notions on how things should be. This can have its own advantages and disadvantageous, especially if both parties have very different views on certain subjects and are unable to comprise satisfactorily.

This is where pre marriage counseling can come in very handy as the couples explore various topics and find some level of acceptance and compromise.

The topic of children is usually an area that presents a lot of challenge and it not tackled well, it will eventually lead to serious problems within the future relationship. This is what the counseling session would ideally like to avoid, thus making it possible to give the couple a better insight to the upbringing and handling of children.

Relationships already have to put up with a lot of other challenges in order to make it work, and having children added to the equation does not make things any easier. In fact it could even be the actual cause of many marriages eventually breaking up.

Therefore it would be wise to explore this particular platform when attending pre marriage counseling sessions. One counseling session would start this particular discussion by encouraging both parties to talk about their childhood and how they were raised.

This would give everyone a better picture of how the individual views children and the general upbringing process. This is a good starting point as the counselor will be able to guide the couple through the various encounters they would most likely have to face as a couple when children are part of the equation.

This is also important when the couple in question have very different views on how things should be done and how the issue of child upbringing should be tacked. Therefore in order to limit any possibility of problems these counseling sessions would be a good place to start the understanding process of children.

Chapter 9- Pre-Marriage Setting Possible Goals and Expectation

Taking as much care as possible to avoid as many pitfalls will help the marriage get off to a good start and stay that way for much of the time. Pre marital counseling is one way to getting off to a good start because at this juncture the couple will learn about almost every different aspect of how to work at a marriage and what they can expect to encounter.

One of the more topics explored would be the one on religion. This of course for most seems to be rather a simple matter and if both parties are not really practicing any particular religion they may not see any real importance in this particular area within the marriage. However for the pre marriage counselor, this is a very important area that should be thoroughly understood for the benefit of both parties and for the eventual well being of the marriage and future children the couple would intend to have.

The aim here is to create some level of clear understanding and respect for all the various religious elements so that both parties will be better able to avoid any future conflicts that may arise successfully and without damaging the relationship in any significant way.

This is especially important for those intending to be part of, or are already in an interfaith relationship. This particular type of relationship has the potential of presenting even more problem than any other normal relationship, thus needing even more pre marital counseling care and guidance. In the initial stages both parties will not be able to understand the possible impacts of being in an interfaith relationship, but as time goes by it may become more difficult to cohabitate peacefully and happily while still wanting to practice one's own religious beliefs, thus the need to explore and discuss matters pertaining to religion openly.

Rules

As with every endeavor, marriage also require some ground rules in which both parties are expected to commit to for the betterment of the relationship.

The process of establishing such ground rules should ideally be done as a couple and if possible with the added help of an experienced pre marriage counselor.

This is very useful as it will help both parties go into the relationship with a clear understanding of what is expected of them both.

The following are some areas that should be covered by the ground rules to ensure the relationship stays the best it can be:

Laying down the perimeters of acceptable behavior and unacceptable behavior, would be a good place to start. Although both parties already have some idea of each other's personalities, the boundaries are necessary to ensure what is presently considered normal does not change in anyway and where unpleasant surprises are the call of the day.

Other ground rules should ideally cover the topic of finances. This very delicate matter is usually the main cause of problems within any existing relationship and without the ground rules in place, there would really be no guidelines to follow to ensure conflicts are kept at bay. Understanding the spending habits and commitments of both parties and learning how to reach compromises will help both parties eventually accept each other's financial commitments and needs, thus creating a clearer picture of what to expect in the future.

Communicating is another very important ground rule to establish very early on in the relationship. Being able to communicate freely and openly should be something that insisted upon as this will give both parties a chance to be honest and forthcoming with their own thoughts and feelings within the relationship.

Discussing expectations

Every human being has aspirations in life, and while some are quite detailed and extensive other may not really have that much to aspire about. However everyone should be given the opportunity to pursue such expectations without any outside pressure or discouragement.

The Seed of Marriage

For those who are lucky enough to have a clear picture of their expectations, finding someone who will fit the profile would be one way of going about choosing the ideal partner.

However for most people who tend to go with the flow, it might be harder to eventually be more firm with their expectations in the relationship.

The importance of expectations being expressed very early on in the relationship cannot be emphasized enough. This will allow both parties to be aware of the expectations, so that they can decide if they can be part of such expectations or if they would prefer to move on to another relationship more fitting to their agenda.

Expectations are often good guiding tools to have as long as they don't become a dominating and uncompromising factor in an individual's life. With expectations in place the individual is better able to adjust and also get the other party to understand the stand taken on certain elements.

A pre marriage counselor will be able to guide both parties on the way to decide and document these expectations in a more logical and realistic way, thus giving both parties an insight of what to expect within the relationship and its future direction.

Discussing these expectations will also allow both parties to be in sync once it is agreed that the expectations are acceptable. There will be less conflict and more working in tandem to ensure the expectations of both parties are adequately met within the confines of the relationship.

Marriage is difficult enough to cope with, without being burdened with unnecessary elements that would cause conflict and negativity. In order to limit these negative outside elements and to ensure a better marriage relationship, it would be good for both parties to explore potentially problematic issue before actually taking the very important step towards a more permanent relationship in the form of marriage.

One of the more difficult dangers to face would be the idea of divorce when things don't go as planned, however most couple do try to hold on as long as possible, but if these issues are not resolved divorce would still be inevitable.

Most pre marriage counselors would usually advice the couple to take a very serious attitude to the various topics often explored through the course of the counseling sessions.

These topics are often very pivotal in ensuring the best mindsets are created, in order to be able to withstand the pressure caused by situations within the topics explored.

Failing to understand the importance of a pre marriage counseling session and take action to join such sessions will only cause the couple to be less equipped to deal with the pressures of marriage.

Other dangers would include having to endure an unhappy marriage situation without positive alternative or escapes available. This will eventually take a toll on the individual's mental and physical wellbeing. In some cases the results from a bad marriage can be so extensive that one party will often resort to unthinkable ways to get out of the seemingly desperate situation with little or no regards for its consequences. This is a very sad option to follow especially when there are now children included in the equation of the family unit.

About the Author

Andrea Clarkson is a mother of four and is married for 29 years. Her married life is a roller coaster ride but she is proud to say that they are able to embrace every challenge and surpass everything as a family.

Andrea Clarkson is a known family counselor and has helped hundreds of family. Now, Andrea wants to help more family and those who are planning to build a family of their own by writing this book. Andrea and her family live in Oregon.